AN APPLE FOR
MY TEACHER

By
Melody Carlson

Honor Books
Tulsa, Oklahoma

An Apple for My Teacher
ISBN 1-56292-661-6
Copyright © 2001 by Melody Carlson

Published by Honor Books
P.O. Box 55388
Tulsa, Oklahoma 74155

AN APPLE FOR
MY TEACHER

By
Melody Carlson

Dedication

For all those teachers who've made a difference
in my life: Mrs. Denning, Mrs. Newman, Mr.
Batch, Mr. Lamb, Mr. Hanley, Mrs. Hagebush,
Mrs. Morin, Mr. Mortenson, Mrs. Young. And
the thousands of others who touch the hearts and
minds of young people daily.

PRESENTATION PAGE

Dear _____,

How do I say thanks for all that you do? Day after day you're here for me. You greet me each morning with a sunny smile and send me home each day with lots of great new ideas bubbling in my head. *You make coming to school fun!*

And since I can't give you a *real* apple every day (I don't have that many apples!), I hope this "little apple book" will bring words to brighten each day of your school year. Because I know that even though I think you're the greatest teacher ever, you're job isn't always easy and there are days when you could use a little encouragement—in just the same way you encourage me!

Thanks for being my teacher!

_____

TABLE OF CONTENTS

3 SPRING BLOSSOMS

A good teacher remembers what it was like to be taught by their favorite teacher.

—ROBERT MCLAIN

AUTUMN DREAMS

A time of gathering back together

Eager minds, young hearts, fresh voices

Warm and slightly weary from summer

Yet full of unexpressed hopes and dreams

And bright expectations of what lies ahead

School is back in session!

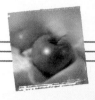

You Are
a Teacher!

——— • ———

Have you ever had one of those end-of-summer, pre-school-year nightmares where buckets of purple paint spill from the ceiling and three-headed "children" speak to you in foreign tongues? But suddenly you wake up and remember that *you are a teacher* and school is about to start! Although there may be challenges in the classroom, thankfully, they will be nothing like your pre-school-year nightmares. And because you're a teacher, you're up for the challenge.

But as the day grows closer, a sense of hope and anticipation begins to sweep over you. You wonder how many children will be in your class this year. Will there be a couple of geniuses amidst the bunch? A class clown? A child with wide eyes who's too shy to speak? You think about the children who will soon become your new little friends, who will look up to you with love and admiration—with great expectation. Simply because *you are a teacher!*

It's a time of hopeful wonder, mixed with the realization that there will also be trials and struggles ahead. Perhaps a parent who's difficult, a child who's suffered abuse, or one with behavioral problems. You know what to expect because it's all just part of the teaching life.

And yet, you look forward to it, because *you are a teacher!* You are ready to take on these challenges and transform them into bright successes. You have a sharp mind and a caring heart—not to mention a witty sense of humor. *For you are a teacher!*

You appreciate the value of the young lives that have been entrusted to you. And you realize the investment you are making in the future. You don't take these responsibilities lightly. Yet you know how to laugh and have fun. When the going gets tough, you know how to pray.

FOR YOU ARE A TEACHER!

Teaching is a rigorous act of faith.

—SUSAN OHANIAN

15

THE TIME
HAS COME

═══ • ═══

Anticipation building
The bulletin board is up
The pungent smell of clean and shining floors
Desks squared off into neat rows
A new school year about to begin!

Hopes, desires, expectations . . .
Young minds, like sponges, eager to learn
Thirsting for knowledge
(whether they know it or not).
A silent prayer upon my heart:
Teach me to teach—again.

AN APPLE A DAY

(RECIPE FOR AN EXCELLENT TEACHER)

A is for aptitude—intelligence to teach.
P is for patience—when they're hard to reach.
P is for prayer—when my day's work is done.
L is for love—may I love *everyone!*
E is for empathy—a feeling heart.

MIX THEM TOGETHER
AND WE CAN START!

17

Once children learn how to learn,
nothing is going to narrow their minds.
The essence of teaching is to make learning
contagious, to have one idea spark another.

—MARVA COLLINS

WHY GOD CREATED
TEACHERS

═══ • ═══

When God created teachers,
He gave us special friends
To help us understand His world
And truly comprehend
The beauty and the wonder
Of everything we see,
And become a better person
With each discovery.

When God created teachers,
He gave us special guides
To show us ways in which to grow
So we can all decide

How to live and how to do
What's right instead of wrong,
To lead us so that we can lead
And learn how to be strong.

Why God created teachers,
In His wisdom and His grace,
Was to help us learn to make our world
A better, wiser place.

—Unknown

First-Impression Prayer

═══ ● ═══

May I smile at each new student
And remember each new name.
May I make each child feel special,
And know they're not the same.

May my words be kind and patient,
And the best that they can be.
Please help my first impression
To reflect the love in me.

Amen.

═══ ● ═══

Education's purpose is to replace
an empty mind with an open one.

—MALCOLM S. FORBES

Teacher's Blessing

May my class size be manageable,
And my recess duties light.
May my parents be supportive,
And my principal kind and understanding.

And if all else fails:
May I grow in wisdom and patience each day
And may summer come quickly!

═══ • ═══

*A teacher who is indeed wise does not
bid you to enter the house of his wisdom,
but rather leads you to the threshold of your mind.*
—KAHLIL GIBRAN

TIMELESS TIDBITS OF WISDOM

*You cannot teach anyone anything.
You can only help them to discover it within themselves.*

—GALILEO

*I will never let my schooling
get in the way of my education.*

—MARK TWAIN

*It is the supreme art of the teacher to awaken joy
in creative expression and knowledge.*

—ALBERT EINSTEIN

*"You address me as 'Teacher' and 'Master,'
and rightly so. That is what I am. So if I,
the Master and Teacher, washed your feet,
you must now wash each other's feet. I've laid
down a pattern for you. What I've done, you do."*

—JESUS CHRIST

John 13:13-15 THE MESSAGE

SEEING DEEPER

Oh, that I might realize
What it is that makes each child tick.
May I not see by sight alone,
Or pass a judgment—too quick.

May I listen, watch, and wait,
View them through their Maker's eyes,
So my teaching reaches deeper,
As I learn to be more wise.

═══ ● ═══

Every child is an artist.
The problem is how to remain
an artist once he grows up.
—PABLO PICASSO

23

THE MIRACLE OF THE
BEGINNING READER

———— • ————

I wriggle and I jiggle,
And I rock upon my chair.
I wiggle a loose tooth,
And I twirl a strand of hair.

I chew on several fingers,
And I sometimes suck my thumb.
I tap the reading table
Like I'd play upon a drum.

I kick my foot with rhythm,
And lose the place where I should look.
I rub my nose and clear my throat,
And sometimes drop my book.

I look outside the window,
And I look down at the floor.
I pay very close attention
When someone's at the door.

I close my eyes and rest my head,
My teacher's heart must bleed.
But in spite of all of this,
I'm learning how to read!

—Unknown

25

> *The whole art of teaching is only the art of*
> *awakening the natural curiosity of young minds*
> *for the purpose of satisfying it afterwards.*
> —ANATOLE FRANCE

TWICE AND AGAIN

— ● —

Most will agree that the ability to teach *really* well is a rare gift indeed. And, certainly, not just anyone can stand up before a crowded classroom and impart understandable knowledge to a bunch of squirming kids. It requires practice, perseverance, and patience to present meaningful lessons—day after day, year after year. And it takes intelligence, substance, and skill to make education practical and memorable for your students. And then there are always those challenging moments when a teacher must call upon the deepest resources—qualities like humor, honesty, mercy, and love.

But the sad truth is, not all teachers are prepared for this demanding task of changing young lives. And yet, what a rare blessing when they are! For as teachers rise to the occasion, they bestow a priceless gift upon their students. And, in fact, they're investing in the future for us all!

So then, what is the secret of a truly great teacher?

What is that hidden edge that some teachers seem to naturally possess?

How is it that some teachers are able to inspire our children to learn, igniting their hunger for knowledge? How did they become so adept and intuitive in their ability to spark a child's interest?

Perhaps it's because they, as teachers, have never stopped being students themselves. Perhaps it's a deep down love for learning that guides them. It could also be their committed respect for knowledge and the understanding that they themselves will never fully arrive, never know it all. Maybe it's that hunger within their hearts for learning that reveals to them new and exciting ways to teach.

If these things are true, a great teacher is doubly blessed! For not only do they experience the thrill of successful teaching, but they also receive the satisfaction of continuing their own academic journey as well.

27

The moment you stop learning, you stop leading.

—RICK WARREN

LET THEM COME

———— • ————

"Let the little children come to Me,
and do not forbid them;
for of such is the kingdom of God.
Assuredly, I say to you, whoever does not receive
the kingdom of God as a little child
will by no means enter it."

—JESUS CHRIST

Luke 18:16–17 NKJV

———— • ————

If the children are untaught, their ignorance and
vices will, in future life, cost us much dearer
in their consequences than it would have
done in their correction by a good education.

—THOMAS JEFFERSON

A WORD FROM
THE WISE

The human mind is not capable of grasping the Universe. We are like a little child entering a huge library. The walls are covered to the ceiling with books in many different tongues. The child knows that someone must have written these books. It does not know who or how. It does not understand the languages in which they are written. But the child notes a definite plan in the arrangement of the books; a mysterious order it does not comprehend, but only dimly suspects.

—ALBERT EINSTEIN

29

CLASSROOM RIDDLES

— ● —

What is warm and fuzzy and has four arms?
A hug!

What is only inches long but contains a mile?
A smile!

What is highly contagious but incredibly healthy?
Laughter!

What is inexpensive to give
but priceless to receive?
Love!

I Shall Not Pass This Way Again

Through this toilsome world, alas!
Once and only once I pass;
If a kindness I may show,
If a good deed I may do
For a suffering fellow man,
Let me do it while I can.
No delay, for it is plain
I shall not pass this way again.

—Unknown

*It is better to build children
than to repair adults.*

—Unknown

A Teacher's Survival Kit

(CAN BE FOUND IN MOST TEACHERS' DESKS)

———— • ————

A Toothpick:
A reminder to point out the
good qualities in all my students.

A Rubber Band:
A reminder to be flexible;
things don't always go as planned.

A Band-Aid:
A reminder that some kids have wounds
and may need my help to heal.

A Pencil:
A reminder to list my daily blessings
and remind my students to do the same.

An Eraser:
A reminder that I am human and
need to forgive and forget mistakes.

A Stick of Gum:
A reminder to "stick" with it and
encourage my students to do likewise.

A Mint:
A reminder that my students are worth
a mint to me (even if I don't get paid one!).

A Candy Kiss:
A reminder that everyone needs lots
of love and hugs and warm squeezes.

A Tea Bag:
A reminder to take time to
relax, unwind, refresh, and refuel.

—Unknown

Teacher's
Serenity Prayer

═══ • ═══

God grant me wisdom, creativity, and love.

With wisdom,
May I look to the future and see the effect
That my teaching will have on these children,
And thus adapt my methods
To fit the needs of each one.

With creativity,
May I prepare new and interesting projects
That challenge my students
And expand their minds to set higher goals
And dream loftier dreams.

With love,
May I praise my students for jobs well done
And encourage them to get up
And go on when they fail.
Lord, reveal Yourself through me.

Amen.

—Unknown

*Children are the messages
we will send to a time we never see.*
—NEIL POSTMAN

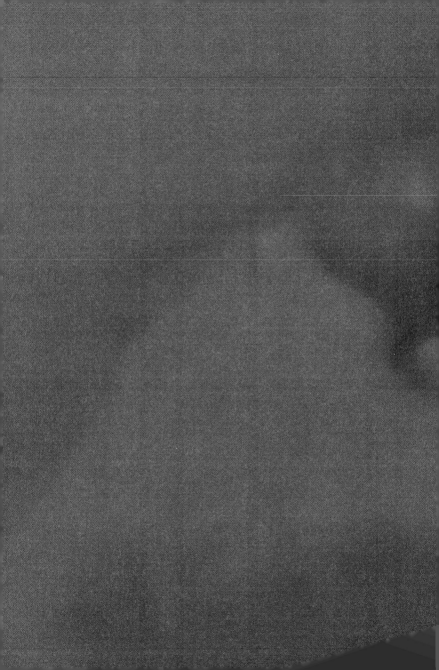

SECTION TWO

WINTER WORKS

A quiet busyness fills the classroom
Little heads bowed low
Engrossed in active learning
Working hard
With eyes, hands, fingers, tongue
All focused on the task
As they are busily becoming
What it is they'll someday be.

A TRULY HONORABLE
PROFESSION

===== ● =====

As children, we usually either disdained them or looked up to them with awe and respect. We may have drawn derogatory stick-men pictures behind their backs or silently admired them from afar. But it was impossible not to be affected and impacted by those who taught us. And if, as it turned out, we chose to join them in this strange and often maligned profession (this mysterious field of education), we probably knew that it wouldn't be easy—nor were we in it "for the money."

And yet, we need to remember that it truly is an honorable profession. Perhaps not on Wall Street or in the Fortune 500. But over the long haul, when the things that really matter are all added up and accounted for—maybe by then everyone will realize that all good teachers are truly worth their weight in gold. But in the meantime, we might struggle with things like identity, job-related stress, self-worth, personal validation. But this struggle is only temporary.

For the time will surely come when all values of Heaven and earth will be turned upside down. And the things that really mattered all along will be made perfectly plain and clear. Things like the nurturing and educating of young minds. Things like love and grace and forgiveness; a helping hand along life's way. And those godly teachers who poured out their hearts and souls into caring for and serving children will be honored. For you see, teaching truly is an honorable profession.

> *"Do not lay up for yourselves treasures on earth, where moth and rust destroy and where thieves break in and steal; but lay up for yourselves treasures in heaven, where neither moth nor rust destroys and where thieves do not break in and steal. For where your treasure is, there your heart will be also."*
>
> —JESUS CHRIST
>
> Matthew 6:19-21 NKJV

THE MIRACLE OF
LEARNING

Like a seed planted some time ago
Lying in the cold winter ground
Nearly forgotten
So many lessons rest, dormant, waiting.

But then, something happens.
A ray of warmth, a sprinkling of understanding
And, lo, the seed begins to awaken,
Stretching out tender roots, exploring.

Then with a burst of revelation,
The tender bud shoots forth,
Lifting up its face victorious
Toward the light.
And the miracle of learning has begun.

How Do You SPELL PATIENCE?

Power to exercise self-control
Allow some things to roll off
Time to take a break
Interest to be given
Energy to think
Never make a stink
Care for a young friend
Even this day will end!

═══ ● ═══

If the only tool you have is a hammer,
you tend to see every problem as a nail.

—ABRAHAM MASLOW

WHOSE CHILD
IS THIS?

━━━ ● ━━━

"Whose child is this?" I asked one day,
Seeing a little one out at play.
"Mine," said the parent with tender smile.
"Mine to keep a little while.
To bathe his hands and comb his hair
To tell him what he is to wear.
To prepare him that he may always be good
And each day do the things he should."

"Whose child is this?" I asked again.
As the door opened and someone came in.
"Mine," said the teacher with
   the same tender smile.
"Mine, to keep for a little while.

To teach him how to be gentle and kind,
To train and direct his dear little mind,
To help him live by every rule,
And get the best he can from school."

"Whose child is this?" I asked once more,
Just as the little one entered the door.
"Ours," said the parent and the teacher,
    they smiled.
Each took a hand of the little child.
"Ours, to love and train together,
Ours, this blessed task, forever."

—Unknown

PRAYER FOR WISDOM

━━━━ ● ━━━━

Dear Lord, as I begin this day,
Make me wise, oh Lord, I pray.
Show me ways to understand
The children placed within my hand.

Lord, I need Your help to learn
How to teach and to discern
What is good and right and true.
Sometimes I don't have a clue.

Dear Lord, I need Your help to see
The needs of those all around me.
I need Your wisdom, Lord, to teach;
To touch a mind, a heart to reach.

Amen.

━━━━ ● ━━━━

*The philosophy of the schoolroom in one generation
will be the philosophy of government in the next.*

—ABRAHAM LINCOLN

CAN YOU SEE ME?

I'm in your class, well, most of the time anyway.
Sometimes I don't make it (cuz, well,
  stuff happens).
But sometimes, in your class, I'm invisible.
No one—not you, not the kids—can see me.
And sometimes I imagine I'm super-powered
  and I can fly
Far, far away from here
From everything and everyone that hurts me.
But I can't, not really. I can't fly.
Maybe it's because I'm too stupid
Or too slow or too dumb.
That's what some people say,
And maybe they're right.
I don't know for sure
But can *you* see me?

═══ • ═══

He who opens a school door closes a prison.

—VICTOR HUGO

LEARNING NEVER ENDS

———— • ————

*Anyone who stops learning is old, whether at twenty
or eighty. Anyone who keeps learning stays young.*
—HENRY FORD

I cannot teach you; only help you to explore yourself.
—BRUCE LEE

*It's not who you are that holds you back,
it's who you think you're not.*
—UNKNOWN

We teach best that which we most need to learn.
—RICHARD BACH

*Give instruction to the wise,
and they will become wiser still;
teach the righteous and they will gain in learning.*

—Proverbs 9:9 NRSV

TEACHING UNIQUENESS

Each second we live is a new and unique moment of the universe, a moment that never was before and will never be again. And what do we teach our children in school? We teach them that two and two makes four and that Paris is the capital of France. When will we also teach them what they are? You should say to each of them: Do you know what you are? You are unique. In all the world there is no other child exactly like you. In the millions of years that have passed, there has never been a child like you. And look at your body—what a wonder it is! Your legs, your arms, your cunning fingers, the way you move! You may be a Shakespeare, a Michelangelo, a Beethhoven. You have the capacity for anything. Yes, you are a marvel.

—Pablo Cassals

ODE TO A MUCH
LOVED TEACHER

━━━ ● ━━━

Just as I was ready to give up
On ever learning anything at all,
I landed in a caring teacher's class;
A man who seemed to clearly know his call.

This teacher understood a line of prose,
Had passion for a fine, well written book;
At home with Robert Frost and Jack London,
He made his students take a second look.

And so instead of simply giving up,
I found myself enticed to *want* to learn—
To read, to write, to study all I could;
The hunger in me soon began to burn.

I quickly found that there was much to know!
My teacher couldn't dish it out too fast!
But perhaps the best thing that he taught
Was learning, once begun, will always last.

> *I cannot teach anybody anything,*
> *I can only make them think.*
>
> —SOCRATES

WHAT YOU DON'T KNOW
COULD BLESS YOU

━━━ ● ━━━

Every single day is a new opportunity to touch the life of a child in a meaningful and memorable way. Yet so often, teachers, pressed by schedules and recess duty and aptitude tests and interruptions, often lose sight of such significant moments. They strive to do the task before them, care for the needs of their students, impart a little learning, and it's possible they don't even notice some of the impact they are making.

But little eyes are watching. And young hearts are being affected on a regular basis. And the teacher who is diligently going about the work of teaching is probably touching lives in a multitude of ways that he or she may never even be aware of. And, yet, it happens. Every school year and possibly every day.

The proof that it happens is tucked safely in all the stories that veteran school teachers happen to hear (years after the fact, of course). It happens when Mrs. Johnson meets thirty-three-year-old Jenny White in the grocery store. And Jenny gushes, "You'll never know how much it meant to me that time you sent a note home to my step mom, telling her how helpful I'd been." Or when Mr. Davis runs into Jason Oleander (the boy he felt would surely end up in prison), who now looks crisp and neat in his three-piece suit. "Mr. Davis, have I ever thanked you for the way you encouraged me in arithmetic? I'm a CPA now, and I always give all the credit to my fifth-grade math teacher."

Consider all the stories teachers never hear. For each story shared, there must be millions that go untold. But the impact on society and the gratitude of many remain just the same. And teachers can be sure there are many, many success stories they will never hear or know. But then gratitude isn't the reason they're teaching, is it?

> *The object of teaching a child is to enable them to get along without their teacher.*
>
> —ELBERT HUBBARD

You're Someone Special

═══ ● ═══

Someone special is someone
Who thinks of those in need
And brings a bit of sunshine
With every caring deed.

Someone special is someone
Whose sharing makes them part
Of all the treasured memories
That are precious to the heart.

Someone special is someone
Who spreads happiness wherever they go,
A special blessing to the world
And a special joy to know.

—Unknown

═══ ● ═══

Everything should be made as simple
as possible, but not simpler.
—Albert Einstein

WHAT STUDENTS NEED

Students do not need to be labeled or measured by more than they are. They don't need more federal funds, grants, and gimmicks. What they need from us is common sense, dedication, and bright, energetic teachers who believe that all children are achievers and who take personally the failure of any one child.

—Marva Collins

53

A teacher who can arouse a feeling
for one single good action,
for one single good poem,
accomplishes more than he who fills our memory
with rows on rows of natural objects,
classified with name and form.

—JOHANN WOLFGANG VON GOETHE

TEACHERS

Teachers are full of patience.
Teachers never give up
And won't let you give up either.
Teachers take students seriously.
Teachers care in their sleep.
Teachers see the genius
In every drawing, poem, and essay.
Teachers make you feel important.
Teachers also help others.
Teachers never grow old.
Teachers stay famous in their students' minds,
Forever.

—Unknown Student Author

A Morning Blessing

May God bless you this day
As you rush on your way
Embracing this life that you live.

May your spirits be bright
And your burdens be light
May your heart be preparing to give.

May discernment abound
And all wisdom be found
With common sense along the way.

May a smile light your face
And your speech be with grace
As you bless those you teach on this day.

A Good "Tool Box"

Love = the glue that holds everything together
Joy = the box of brilliant crayons that color
   our world with wonder
Peace = the ruler to measure our lives by
Patience = the pencil that can always
   be resharpened
Gentleness = the soft tissues that wipe
   away tears
Kindness = the pink pearl eraser that
   removes mistakes
Self-Control = the scissors that cut away
   harsh edges
Endurance = the tennis shoes that are ready
   to run and run!

GIFTED TEACHERS

What happens when we live God's way?
He brings gifts into our lives, much the
same way that fruit appears in an orchard—
things like affection for others,
exuberance about life, serenity.
We develop a willingness to stick with things,
a sense of compassion in the heart, and
a conviction that a basic holiness
permeates things and people.
We find ourselves involved in loyal commitments,
not needing to force our way in life, able
to marshal and direct our energies wisely.

—Galatians 5:22–23 THE MESSAGE

57

TAKE TIME

— ● —

Take time to work, it is the price of success.
Take time to think, it is the source of power.
Take time to play, it is the secret of
  perpetual youth.
Take time to read, it is the foundation
  of wisdom.
Take time to be friendly, it is the road
  to happiness.
Take time to dream, it is hitching your
  wagon to a star.
Take time to love and be loved, it is the
  privilege of the saints.
Take time to look around, it is too short
  a day to be selfish.
Take time to laugh, it is the music of the soul.

—Old English Prayer

58

A TIME-TESTED PRAYER

*Oh, that You would bless me indeed, and enlarge
my territory, that Your hand would be with me,
and that You would keep me from evil,
that I may not cause pain!*

THE PRAYER OF JABEZ

1 Chronicles 4:10 NKJV

*A helping word to one in trouble
is often like a switch on a railroad track . . .
an inch between wreck and smooth,
rolling prosperity.*

—HENRY WARD BEECHER

BELIEVE

Believe in yourself,
In the power you have
To control your own life
Day by day.

Believe the strength
That you have deep inside
Will help you show the way.

Believe in tomorrow
And what it will bring.
Let a hopeful heart
Carry you through.

For things will work out
If you trust and believe.
There's no limit to
What you can do!

—Unknown

THE RIPPLING EFFECT

Drop a stone into the water—
In a moment it is gone.
But there are a hundred ripples
Circling on and on and on—
Say a word of cheer and splendor—
In a moment it is gone
But there are a hundred ripples
Circling on and on.

—Unknown

Train up a child in the way he should go,
And when he is old he will not depart from it.

—Proverbs 22:6 NKJV

HAND IN HAND
WITH GOD

━━━ ● ━━━

When God is our companion
As we walk the road of life,
There is help for every problem,
And grace for care and strife,
And we'll find that we've been happy
All along the path we've trod,
When, in faith, we've made the journey,
Hand in hand along with God.

—Unknown

MORE TIMELESS TIDBITS

Teaching should be full of ideas, not stuffed with facts.
—UNKNOWN

A teacher affects eternity; he can never tell where his influence stops.
—HENRY ADAMS

Education is not filling a bucket, but lighting a fire.
—WILLIAM BUTLER YEATS

You can teach a lesson for a day, but if you teach curiosity, you teach for a lifetime.
—UNKNOWN

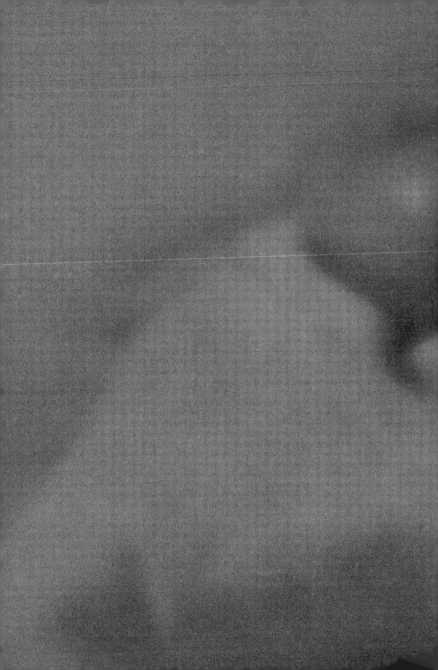

SPRING BLOSSOMS

Those little seeds of learning have germinated
Warmed by the sunlight of knowledge
Watered by wise words of instruction
Nurtured by loving acts of kindness
Strong young minds,
like eager seedling evergreens
Now stretch eagerly toward
the light of understanding
Growing strong and tall and sturdy
And able to stand on their own.

REMEMBER THE
CHILD WITHIN

===== ● =====

How can we expect to truly reach children, transform fresh minds, touch young hearts, inspire real learning—if we can't remember what it was like to be a child? If we have become so caught up in our "grown-up" responsibilities that we lose touch with that little girl, that little boy, who is tucked somewhere deep within us, unless we can relate to childhood, how can we expect to connect with *real* children?

Can you remember dour-faced teachers who seemed older than Methuselah? The kind who'd always watch for a kid to blow it—one mistake and they'd let 'em have it—and good? Can you recall anything childlike about one of those teachers? Anything that connected with your own youth, spontaneity, and free spirit? Probably not. And most likely those are not the types of teachers who inspired you to teach in the first place, unless it was to convince you that you could do it better.

But somehow, it's easy to get caught up in the adult world and forget what it is like to be child.

Easy to forget that we don't *really* have all the answers. Easy to neglect to ask those fresh and challenging questions. Easy to not try new things or welcome different experiences. Easy to stifle curiosity by choosing to stick with the tried and true. Easy to play it safe. And before you know it, you could become old and stuffy, just like those teachers you never liked.

Worst of all, you could lose that sweet, simple joy of everyday living.

If this has happened to you, remember that it's never too late. Unlike many of your adult peers (who work around grown-ups all day), you have a built in "anti-aging" protective barrier. Take a good, long look at those little lives all around you—study them and remember what it's like to be young. Soon you will be able to welcome your own "child" back to the surface. And you can, once again, laugh and play and celebrate the freshness of life!

What a blessing it is to be linked, hand in hand, with children!

67

He who is afraid to ask is ashamed of learning.

—DANISH PROVERB

HOW TO STAY FOREVER YOUNG

— • —

Youth is not a time of life,
It is a state of mind.
You are as old as your doubt, your fear, your despair.
The way to keep young
Is to keep your faith young.
Keep your self-confidence young.
Keep your hope young.

—LUELLA F. PHEAN

Those who wait on the LORD
Shall renew their strength;
They shall mount up with wings like eagles,
They shall run and not be weary,
They shall walk and not faint.

—Isaiah 40:31 NKJV

How Do You Spell Teacher?

T is for *tolerance, thoughtfulness,* and *tenderness*—to show the gentle way.

E is for *enthusiasm, excitement,* and *energy*—to brighten up the day.

A is for *aptitude, ability,* and *action*—the skills to see you through.

C is for *caring, comfort,* and *charity*—in all you say and do.

H is for *helpful, happy,* and *handy*—with these you can't go wrong.

E is for *equity, empathy, encouragement*—to help kids get along.

R is for *resourceful, responsible, reasonable*—you just can't get enough.

So, that's how you spell *teacher*—one who's made of the right stuff!

——— ● ———

You can pay people to teach,
but you can't pay them to care.

—MARVA COLLINS

HUGS

It's wondrous what a hug can do
A hug can cheer you when you're blue
A hug can say, "I love you so!"
Or, "Gee, I hate to see you go."

A hug can soothe a small child's pain
And bring a rainbow after rain.
The HUG—there's just no doubt about it—
We scarcely could survive without it.

Hugs are great for fathers and mothers,
Sweet for sisters, as well as brothers.
Chances are some favorite aunt
Loves them more than potted plants.

Kittens crave them,
Puppies love them,
Heads of state
Are not above them.

A hug can break the language barrier,
And make the dullest day seem merrier.
No need to fret about the store of 'em.
The more you give, there's only more
  of 'em.

So stretch those arms without delay,
And give someone a hug today!

—Unknown

In My Lifetime

———— • ————

In my lifetime
I hope to develop
Arms that are strong
Hands that are gentle
Ears that will listen
Eyes that are kind
A mind full of wisdom
A heart that understands
A tongue that will speak softly.

—UNKNOWN

The process of learning requires
not only hearing and applying but also
forgetting and then remembering again.

—JOHN GRAY

LOVE FINDS
A WAY

I am done with great things and big plans,
great institutions and big success.
I am for those tiny, invisible, loving
   human forces
that work from individual to individual,
creeping through the crannies of the world
like so many rootlets,
or like the capillary oozing of water,
which, if given time, will rend the hardest
   monuments of pride.

—William James

TEACHABLE MOMENTS

— ● —

Sometimes you have a *perfect* plan
For how the day should start,
But despite all your efforts
The whole thing falls apart.

Perhaps it is a missing link
Or something very small,
But soon you know your lesson planned
Will never work at all!

But think about the ruined plans
Of a flustered miner of old;
He never saw a speck of tin—
Instead, he found real gold!

So take a breath and look around,
Then say a silent prayer,
And perhaps you'll find the answer tucked
Within the problem there.

> *Vision is the ability to see God's presence,*
> *plan, and power over obstacles.*
>
> —MIKE BREAUX

"RANDOM" ACTS
OF KINDNESS

━━━━ ● ━━━━

In years to come a child may forget
what you taught him, but he will
always remember how you made him feel.

—UNKNOWN

The secret of education is respecting the pupil.

—RALPH WALDO EMERSON

People don't care how much you know,
until they know how much you care!

—UNKNOWN

There is never enough time to do or say
all the things that we would wish; the thing is to
do as much as you can in the time that you have.

—CHARLES DICKENS

LEAVE SOMETHING
BEHIND

Spread love everywhere you go;
First of all, in your own house,
Give love to your children,
To your wife or husband,
To a next door neighbor. . . .
Let no one ever come to you without
    leaving better or happier.
Be the living expressions of
    God's kindness,
Kindness in your face,
Kindness in your eyes,
Kindness in your smile,
Kindness in your warm greetings.

—Mother Teresa

SEIZE THE DAY!

—— • ——

The grass is green, the birds are singing,
With bees and flowers and butterflies out.
But inside the school, it's hot and muggy,
With kids distracted and prowling about.

Perhaps it's time to get creative,
To open the windows of your mind.
And take the science project outdoors;
To look and see what you can find!

For each day has some wisdom in it;
Something new to celebrate!
But be aware, or you might miss it,
Stuck inside, one day too late.

For we don't know what comes tomorrow—
Rainy skies or aptitude tests?
So, let's learn to seize the moment,
For *life* lessons are the best!

To teach is to learn again!
—OLIVER WENDELL HOLMES

NO REGRETS

———— • ————

As the school year winds down (or up, depending on your perspective), do you begin to wonder—did I do enough? Did I reach out enough? Did Jenny make enough progress? Did Johnny learn to read well enough? Did I really connect with my class? Will they remember this year with fondness? Should I have done something differently?

And all these doubts, though troubling, only show how much you care. And caring is where good education always begins. But, to be perfectly honest, how is it possible to really measure your effectiveness as a teacher? CAT scores? Teacher evaluations? Test scores can be skewed, and children can act up while their teacher is being observed. So, how will you know if your year was a real success?

Perhaps there's no sure way to be absolutely certain how we rate as teachers. So maybe it would be best to learn to tune in to that quiet, small voice that whispers words of sweet assurance somewhere deep inside of us. That voice that might be saying, "Well done, good servant." Or perhaps we need to embrace a bit of faith and believe that if we did our very best, then someday, somehow, good will spring forth from it.

In truth, the best way to know if we've succeeded is to look at the faces of those who've been in our care. Children aren't usually that good at hiding their feelings. And if those faces are happy and smiling and ignited, then chances are we've done a great job. And so, let's have no regrets. We must remember that we're still learning too, and there's always next year to become even better!

> *If your plan is for 1 year, plant rice.*
> *If your plan is for 10 years, plant trees.*
> *If your plan is for 100 years, educate children.*
>
> —CONFUCIUS

It Takes
Just One

One song can spark a moment,
One flower can wake the dream.
One tree can start a forest,
One bird can herald the spring.

One smile begins a friendship,
One handclasp lifts a soul.
One star can guide a ship at sea,
One word can frame the goal.

One vote can change a nation,
One sunbeam lights a room.
One candle wipes out darkness,
One laugh will conquer gloom.

One step must start each journey,
One word must start each prayer.
One hope will raise our spirits,
One touch can show you care.

One voice can speak with wisdom,
One heart can know what's true.
One life can make the difference,
You see, it's up to YOU!

—Unknown

To teach is to touch a life forever.

—UNKNOWN

To Think Upon

=== ● ===

In a completely rational society, the best of us would aspire to be teachers and the rest would have to settle for something less, because passing civilization along from one generation to the next ought to be the highest honor and highest responsibility anyone could have.

—LEE IACOCCA

The mediocre teacher tells.
The good teacher explains.
The superior teacher demonstrates.
The great teacher inspires.

—WILLIAM ARTHUR WARD

There are no hands so small that they cannot make a difference in the world.

—UNKNOWN

A Day
WELL SPENT

If you sit down at set of sun
And count the acts that you have done,
And counting find
One self-denying deed, one word
That eased the heart of him who heard;
One glance most kind
That fell like sunshine where it went—
Then you may count that day well spent.

—George Eliot

Our job is not to straighten each other out,
but to help each other up.

—NEVA COLE

SLOW DANCE

Have you ever watched kids
On a merry-go-round,
Or listened to rain
Slapping the ground?

Ever followed a butterfly's erratic flight,
Or gazed at the sun as it fades into night?

You'd better slow down, don't dance so fast,
Time is short, the music won't last.
Do you run through each day on the fly?
When you ask, "How are you?"
Do you hear the reply?

When the day is done,
Do you lie in your bed,
With the next hundred chores
Running through your head?

You'd better slow down, don't dance so fast.
Time is short, the music won't last.
Ever told your child,
We'll do it tomorrow,
And in your haste, not see his sorrow?

Ever lost touch,
Let a good friendship die,
'Cause you never had time
To call and say, "Hi"?

87

You'd better slow down, don't dance so fast.
Time is short, the music won't last.

When you run so fast to get somewhere,
You miss half the fun of getting there.
When you worry and hurry though your day,
It's like an unopened gift—
Thrown away.

Life is not a race.
Do take it slower.
Hear the music
Before the song is over.

—Unknown

My heart is singing for joy this morning.
A miracle has happened!
The light of understanding has shone
upon my little pupil's mind,
And behold, all things are changed.

—ANNE SULLIVAN

THANK YOU!

What's nearer and dearer to a parent's heart
Than a beloved child, so sweet and so smart?
A child that's entrusted over to you,
To lead and to guide the whole year through.

And all that you teach and instruct him to be—
The way that you touch him is how you touch me.
For he is my treasure (sent from God up above)
To nurture and cherish, to discipline in love.

So, how can I thank you for how you've cared,
Molding and shaping this child we have shared?
Mere words can't describe all I'd like to say—
May God bless you and keep you along your way!

I will instruct you and teach you
in the way you should go;
I will counsel you and watch over you.

—Psalm 32:8

AN APPLE

An apple lasts a short time
In the hands of a teacher.
A bit of wisdom lasts a lifetime
In the mind of a child.

—UNKNOWN

About the Author

Through the years, Melody Carlson has worn many hats—from preschool teacher to senior editor. But writing is her first love.

Currently, she is a freelance writer who has written more than sixty books for children, teens, and adults. Several have been honored with awards for writing.

Melody lives in Sisters, Oregon, with her husband and two sons. They enjoy skiing, hiking, and biking in the beautiful Cascade Mountains.

Additional copies of this book
and other titles by Honor Books
are available from your local bookstore.

If you have enjoyed this book, or if it has
impacted your life,
we would like to hear from you.

Please contact us at:

Honor Books
Department E
P.O. Box 55388
Tulsa, Oklahoma 74155
Or by e-mail at *info@honorbooks.com*

Honor Books
Tulsa, Oklahoma